Another Kind Of Poverty
Pupils Drama Book
Grades 3 - 7

By Richard Zhuanginyu

Success

An Author

Richard Zhuanginyu was born on 14 February 1964 in Chegutu Zimbabwe.

PERSONAL ATTRIBUTES: Creative, Self starter and hardworking.

PROFESSIONAL QUALIFICATION: Diploma in Fiction Writing from Success College South Africa and Diploma in Theology from Beacon University.

Diploma Evaluation Procedure: His two Diplomas had undergone assessment and approved by the Ministry of High Education in Harare, Zimbabwe.

COURSES EVALUATION: he has also undergone assessment for his matter skills programs to address the student of the University of Zimbabwe. He has extensive experience as founder, headmaster and teacher at Blakiston Junior Evening School in Milton Park Harare, Zimbabwe

PRESENT EMPLOYER: self author, Registered by the Ministry of Education, Sport, Arts & Culture in Harare, Zimbabwe.

He authored six supplementary pupils reading textbooks.

1. Teaching On How To Write Short Stories and Composition In School **Form 1-6**

2. Free to be You, Punha and Tapiwa English Comprehension and Composition Instruct Pupils Book **Grades 3-7**.

3. Learning to Write Correct English Grammar, Composition and Letter Instruct Pupils Book **Grades 3-7**

4. Children are Happy In Zimbabwe, Pupils Play Book **Grades 3-7**

5. Another Kind of Poverty, Pupils Drama Book, **Grades 3-7**

6. Murume Akange Ari Nyoka, Bhuku Revana Vaduku, **Grades 0,1,2,3.**

Success Publishing House Will Be Reprinting Its Six Published Titles

www.facebook.com/successpublishinghouse

Another Kind Of Poverty
Pupils Drama Book
Grades 3 - 7

Another Kind Of Poverty
Pupils Drama Book
Grades 3 - 7

BY RICHARD ZHUANGINYU
SUCCESS

TEXT PUPILS DRAMA BOOK GRADES 3-7

SUCCESS PUBLISHING HOUSE

zhuanginyurichard@gmail.com

HARARE

ZIMBABWE

© Richard Zhuanginyu 2011

All rights reserved.

No part of this publication may be reproduced in any form, or transmitted in any form, whether electronically, mechanically by photocopying or tape record, without the required written permission of the owner and publisher.

ISBN No.978-0-7974-4387-7

CONTENTS

Episode	**Page**
1. Another Kind of poverty	7
2. Nhamo meets Tigere's family	16
3. Mr. Tavaziva and the Boss	20
4. Mr. Tavaziva tells the story to his family	23
5. Mr. Tavaziva at Chimusoro Farm	27
6. Mr. Tavaziva starts working	34
7. A wondering son	38
Supplementary Dictionary	44
Recommendations	48

UNDERSTANDING READINTG A DRAMA

EPISODE 1

ANOTHER KIND OF POVERTY

REPORTER: Greetings to all viewers out there. We're here today to learn more about impoverished family…to let you in on the background ---- the "Nitti "in poverty. And so---"This is your life" Tigere Dangarembwa! (Fanfare and Applause) Come on up here on stage, (Tigere that's right, it's you! Come on up! (Tigere enters shyly) Keep your head up! Now just turn around here and say "Hi" to all those fine folks in our audience today…

ENTER: Chipo and Tigere

TIGERE: Enters, humming, and has leaves stuck in his hair.

TIGERE: Hi, Chipo

CHIPO: Hid Tigere! Tigere! How's it going? Say, what have you been doing? You've got leaves all over you!

TIGERE: Oh, I've got a new job.

CHIPO: You have? What is it?

TIGERE: Well, I'm cutting grass for a lady down the road.

Chipo: Boy, I bet what's hard work.

Tigere: I'll say it is! It wears me out! There must be millions of leaves in that yard!

Chipo: Why are you doing such a hard job like cutting grass? Couldn't you find anything you would enjoy more?

Tigere: I needed to earn more money and I looked and looked for a job. This is the only job I could find, so I figured it was better than nothing.

Chipo: Yes I guess so, but I don't think I could do a good job with something I don't like.

Tigere: Well, I just make myself do it. Remember once when we talked about how, when you've a problem you can usually find your Master to help you along?

CHIPO: Yes, I remember the time when I was so mad at the new girl down the road! I was really going to get her! But you taught me how to obey my mother "Respect your parents as I respect my family, Tigere said that. I thought about that message so that when I started to get mad and do mean things to the girl, it helped me a lot

ENTER: Tigere and Nhamo

NHAMO: Hey: you children what are you doing .there?

Tigere: Who are you?

NHAMO: I'm a caretaker Nhamo

TIGERE: I'm Tigere Dangarembwa. She is Chipo Dangarembwa. What do? You want here Mr. Nhamo?

NHAMO: I'd like to take care of you.

TIGERE: What kind of story do you want from me?

NHAMO: I'd like you to tell me where you were born.

TIGERE: I was born in Chegutu District on fourteen February – nineteen –sixty – four.

NHAMO: In which country?

TIGERE: Zimbabwe.

NHAMO: Where were you born? By the way, don't you understand English Language? You foolish guy!

TIGERE: I do know a little about that place, Gadzema

NHAMO: Isn't it in Chegutu Township?

TIGERE: No it isn't.

NHAMO: How far is it from the Township?

TIGERE: It's about twelve kilometers.

NHAMO: Do you think it's exactly that distance?

TIGERE: My statement I quite right.

NHAMO: Hey –e; you guy wake up! Will you describe your home?

TIGERE: Oh – o – yes Sir, I 'II describe it just now.

NHAMO: Tell me honestly about your home.

TIGERE: Yes l will my home, where I was born is situated on a hillock. It's a thicket, I mean it's surrounded by small trees. There are three huts, one is unthatched. Their doors are facing South West. And there are two bathing rooms thatched with grass and their doors are facing to the East. Behind them there is a water –way, where bananas are planted, and its yard is hedged by cassava plant.

NHAMO: (Politely) Brother Tigere, will you tell me where you fetch water?

Tigere: (Proudly) yes certainly. Do you see this pathway which these Musasa trees are lining? That's the entrance which leads to a place where water is being collected.

NHAMO: I'd like to go with you, because l want to do a research on your water to see whether it has – some germs.

TIGERE: (Politely) Okay Sir, let's go. (Mr. Nhamo and Tigere started walking. Whilst they were on their way their heads were shaking).

NHAMO: What makes my head shake? (Loud – voice). All the birds which were in the trees started trembling with cold and flew off)

TIGERE: My head is shaking, don't you know! You gentleman what have you been doing just now. Why were you shouting? I'll chase you!

NHAMO: (annoyed) What - Wha-w-h-a-ts wrong? Oh- o- hey-e-e, I was only shouting to the birds.
(Tigere wanted to answer Mr. Nhamo, his tears dropped on his shirt).
Tigere: My shirt is wet what can l do now?
(His eyes were red from anger).

TIGERE: I'll take off my shirt and put it in the sun to make it dry. (He took off his shirt and knelt under the Musasa tree).

TIGERE: (Happily) Now the cold water has entered into my heart. (Mr. Nhamo stared at Tigere).

NHAMO: "Hey "! You short boy where did you put your shirt?

TIGERE: I put it in the sunshine for it to dry.

NHAMO: But you short person don't you think what you are doing? (At that moment Tigere started crying).

TIGERE: Mother: Oh –o-o – we-e – mother- somebody is shouting at me under the Musasa tree near our entrance to the river. (Mr. Nhamo and Tigere are unable to speak to each other for five minutes. At that time the rain started falling with the frightening lightning –thunder-storm -)

NHAMO: Hii-i-hey-e-we-e-what's pattering and making such sound of p-a-tter ring? Now l am going to die. Oh-o- yes. The world is becoming dark. Tigere! What's happening?

TIGERE: You took off your shirt! Don't you know that we broke the law of our tradition? If you have money in your pocket put it under this Musasa tree.

NHAMO: I will put it here. I hope I'll not have any trouble. Well brother Tigere, let's walk to the river. Don't forget to take our shirts which are in the sunshine. (When they started walking a grim loud sound takes place).

NHAMO: What makes such loud sounds?

TIGERE: Don't you hear frogs croaking? There is a river.

NHAMO: Is it flooding?

TIGERE: Yes it is. (They reached the river and Mr. Nhamo laughed at Tigere in a loud voice).

NHAMO: (Laughing) Ha-a-a-ha-a ! Yes. These people drink such dirty water which animals also do. "Tigere" Come here I'd like to tell you how dirty your water is.

TIGERE: (Politely) thank you sir, l am coming. (He was walking slowly, he thought Mr. Nhamo wanted to kill him).

TIGERE: What's happening master?

NHAMO: You see how dirty your water is. Why do you drink such dirty? Water, like animals?

TIGERE: What do you mean, when you say dirty water?

NHAMO: Give me this microscope! Do you see these germs?

TIGERE: Yes Sir, I do see them and this is really dirty water, look how big that frog is master. Nhamo: Yes, it's big that a person can eat it.

TIGERE: Of course, l can eat it because it's fat. I still remember a fat frog which was staying in Mupfure River. It was eating the ants and some of the ants entered into its stomach and started stinging its flesh because it had so much fat.

NHAMO: By the way, what's the name of this river?

Tigere: It's Gadzema River.

NHAMO: Okay, let's return home and visit your family.

TIGERE: (Politely) Thank you master. Whilst the two fellows were walking one of them decided to sing a song).

TIGERE: Master, will we sing a titled "The fifteen bottles of castle beer"

NHAMO: Yes let's sing it. Altogether: Fifteen bottles of castle –beer in the man's chest oh-o-hey –e- we-ee!! And a bottle of rum- Oh-o-hey –e-hey –e –we-ee ! And this is the most beautiful song l have ever heard in my life.

TIGERE: Do you realize that our journey is a little bit…shorter than before?

NHAMO: Yes it is.

TIGERE: Do you still remember a tree under which you put your money?

NHAMO: Yes, I still remember it didn't is that tree which has lots of leaves.

TIGERE: Yes it is. Do you know why this place is silent?

NHAMO: I don't know.

TIGERE: It is silent because it's an ancestral place in our traditional culture.

NHAMO: If I find the place in which l put my money will l see it?

TIGERE: No---you won't get your money anymore.

NHAMO: Let's walk, because l don't like to see funny things which will make me afraid.

TIGERE: Be a brave man don't be afraid of anything.

NHAMO: I hear some crowing of cocks, now I'm very happy how far is it.
Tigere: It is about a kilometer. What makes you happy?

NHAMO: I'm afraid of this forest and now I'm free from danger and l am happy.

TIGERE: Do you know that there are various kinds of animals in this forest?

NHAMO: Listen! A roaring of a lion.

TIGERE: Yes, that's true in this forest the lion is the most dangerous of all the animals.

Nhamo: I recognize those short trees which are lining our huts.

Tigere: Yes, they are called cassava plant, which hedge our yard.

Nhamo: Does that mean we are reaching home?

Tigere: Yes we are. Let us wait outside

EPISODE 1
QUESTIONS TO ANSWER

1. Why was Tigere doing hard work like cutting grass?

    a. Because that is the only job he found.
    b. Because he needed to earn money.
    c. Because it was better than nothing.
    d. Because it was better than sleeping.

2. What did Tigere learn about the law of Zimbabwe?
    a. He learnt to be lazy that is the law of Zimbabwe.
    b. He learnt to work hard at his job that is the law of Zimbabwe.
    c. He learnt to do anything that is the law of Zimbabwe.
    d. He learnt to enjoy the world that is the law of Zimbabwe.

3. What is cassava plant?
    a. Cassava plant is a fruit.
    b. Cassava plant is maize-cob.
    c. Cassava plant is a tree
    . Cassava plant is important food product roots starch and nutritious.

4. Who shout the birds?
    a. A gentleman shouted the birds.
    b. Nhamo shouted the birds.
    c. Tigere shouted the birds.
    d. None of the above.

UNDERSTANDING READING A DRAMA
EPISODE 2
NHAMO MEETS TIGERE 'S FAMIL

ENTER:	Tigere, Nhamo, Tavaziva and
NYARAI:	(The two fellows are outside the yard. Tigere's father is shouting).
TAVAZIVA:	My wife Nyarai! I do not see my beloved son Tigere, do you know where he is?
Nyarai:	I don't know where he has gone. But my husband, it is your duty to look after your son, and l have to look after my daughter.
TAVAZIVA:	(Scolding) you, Ladies always think of drinking you don't care for your children. Look! You have lost my son Tigere. Go –go-o find him find him just now, I want to see him this morning.
NYARAI:	(Politely) my husband, Tavaziva beer doesn't make me forget Children and l tell you that l won't

	stop drinking .
TAVAZIVA:	Don't say this to me! I am your husband who looks after you. If you continue doing that I'll chase you just now. (When his son Tigere heard the word chase, he started knocking).
TIGERE:	Knock, knock.
NYARAI:	Who's knocking? I hope there's somebody outside. Let me call my husband to open the door (Loudly) Mr. Tavaziva!! Go outside our yard, somebody has knocked at the door twice.
TAVAZIVA:	(In fear) Look I have to walk on tip – toe. Who's there? Maybe the rascals. Let me open the door silently, this is the end of my life. Let me push it. (Laughing) How! Ha-a , ha-a-a!, you are my beloved son Tigere.
TIGERE:	Father! This is a respectable gentleman named Mr. Nhamo
TAVAZIVA:	Okay, all of you are my sons get inside this hut, and Mr. Nhamo sit on this stool.
NHAMO:	(Politely) Thank you father Tavaziva.
NYARAI:	(A call) Tigere! Bring water and give it to your friend to drink.
TIGERE:	Okay mother, I'm looking for a clean cup.
Family:	This is our traditional law in Zimbabwe
Nhamo:	(Politely) Father Tavaziva, will you tell me where you were born?
TAVAZIVA:	Yes I will, I was born here in Zimbabwe in nineteen forty –five in the district of Chegutu. Nhamo: Will you tell me your favorite food?
TAVAZIVA:	Yes, I can explain about it to you, do you see those small plant?
Nhamo:	On these are called cassava plants.

TAVAZIVA:	I pick up their leaves and squeeze them. Then l mix them with the groundnuts flour and make some relish out of the mixture, we also eat their roots what are dried on the sun.
NHAMO:	After that, what's your second step?
TAVAZIVA:	I've to taste whether they are delicious when boiled for minutes then mix them with the cooked leaves.
NHAMO:	And what else do you do for your family?
TAVAZIVA:	I always go hunting for birds, hares and fishing.
NHAMO:	That's why your children are healthy and wise, you feed them with good food which builds their Tavaziva: Mr. Nhamo I do appreciate your asking me such questions and from today I will not be unkind to anybody.
NHAMO:	I tell you Father Tavaziva to be free in this world. Look after your family and be careful with your drinking water. I tell you today not to drink uncoiled water. If your children get the disease which damages their kidneys, they will become dull in school. I have done my best for you and for your family too. "GOOD BYE, AND GOOD BYE! THE FAMILY!!"

FAMILY: "(Happily) GOOD BYE! MASTER Nhamo"

EPISODE 2
QUESTIONS TO ANSWER

1. Who scold the Ladies?
   a. The ladies were scolded by Tavaziva.
   b. The ladies were scolded by Nhamo.
   c. The ladies were scolded by Tigere.
   d. The ladies were scolded by Nyarai.

2. Tavaziva's favourite food is_____
   a. Meat
   b. Cabbage
   c. Rape
   d. Cassava plant

3. Tavaziva was born in_____
4.
   a. District of Chegutu
   b. District of Harare
   c. District of Mutare
   d. District of Bulawayo

5. Tavaziva gets food for his family from_____
   a. Hunting the birds, hares and fishing.
   b. Hunting ants, snakes and lions.
   c. Hunting baboons, cats and dogs.
   d. Hunting monkeys, rats and owls

UNDERSTANDING READING A DRAMA
Episode 3

Enter: Tavaziva, Nyarai and Boss.

Nyarai: My husband l am happy after talking with a nice man, he taught me about hygiene. That lesson has intruded into my heart.

Tavaziva: But do not stop doing our traditional culture, l need a cup of seven days beer.

Nyarai: Do you know Tavaziva? It is time to go to work.

Tavaziva: I know more than you. I must first be drunk and then start work.

Children: Father if your boss dismisses you, where will we get food? We will die of hunger.

Tavaziva: I'm a clever man my children, l do know what to do for you. Let me visit the Boss (The man started walking on staggering and singing in a loud voice).

Tavaziva: (Silent) I'm staggering what am l to say to the master? If he sees me doing such monkey business. (When the man was about to reach the Boss, his face become pale).

Boss: Hey-e- you! What do you want here? Time for work is over. Wake up you go and find a vacancy with somebody else, because I don't want my workers to disobey the law of this farm.

Tavaziva: (Politely) Forgive me please master.

Queen: My husband this is your trusted worker. What will you do if you lose him? Where will you get another person who know how to look after chickens?

Boss: I won't forgive him I am giving him two hours to pack and go-oo! And my wife do you know that I'm very angry with your speech?

Queen: Yes, I do know my husband.

Boss: You will make me fight him just – just now! I don't want to see him, he must go-go! There is no excuse!

Tavaziva: (a work) I don't care whether I'll die of hunger. There are many bosses who want the people to work for them. But the only thing I will not do is be friendly with a thief and I don't trust them. They make me poor and steal my clothes. Let me go and tell my family what has happened at work. (Whilst the man was on his way home he was deciding some way of getting money to keep his family).

EPISODE 3
QUESTIONS TO ANSWER

1. What kind of beer is named in the passage?

    a. It is called seven days beer.
    b. It is called chibuku beer.
    c. It is called kachasu beer.
    d. It is called chikokiyana beer.

2. Whose family will die of hunger?

    a. Was Boss's family.
    b. Was Tavaziva's family.
    c. Was Queen's family.
    d. Was Tigere's family.

3. Why Tavaziva loses his job?

    a. Because of drunk.
    b. Because of being lazy
    c. Because of sleeping.
    d. Because of talkative.

4. Who was looking after chicken?

    a. Queen was looking after chicken.
    b. Tavaziva was looking after chicken.
    c. The boss was looking after chicken
    d. Nyarai was looking after chicken

UNDERSTANDING READING A DRAMA
EPISODE 4

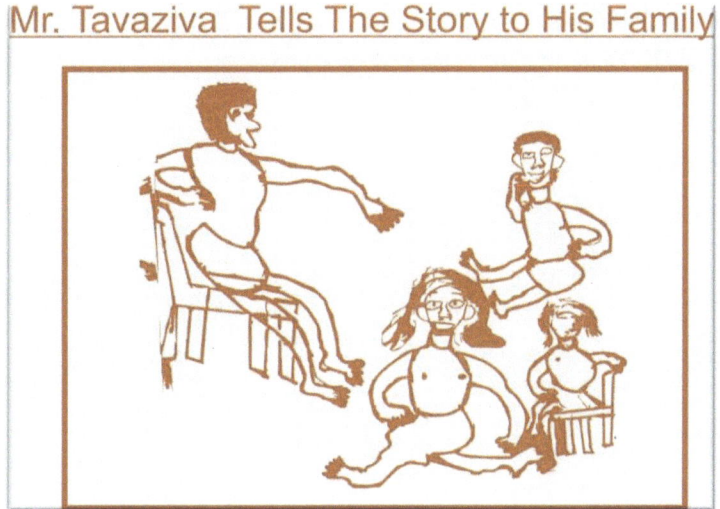

Mr. Tavaziva Tells The Story to His Family

Tavaziva: It seems I'm no help to my family, where will l get money? I am empty handed. I remember l have ten cocks and forty hens, I will put them on sale. (When the man had been working he kept the chickens for his future life. Let us see him meeting his family).

Tavaziva: I will tell you my wife to sell all the chickens and l hope l won't be beholden to anybody. (The man reached home, he stayed outside the yard and peeped in twice).

Tavaziva: These children don't see me! Let me knock at the door, (knock – knock).

Nyarai: Who is knocking, are you a visitor? Why what is happening today?

Tavaziva: Open the door I'm your husband Tavaziva what do you say Nyarai?
Nyarai: You are early today my husband.
Tavaziva: I've left the job and the Boss told me to pack and go which is a terrible message to me.
Children: We told you not to drink so much. Look! Where have we to go? You were laughing at mother and you told her not to drink beer.

Nyarai: Children must respect their father! Don't say such words to your father.

Tavaziva: We must leave the place just now, and I'm telling you to collect all clothes because we are leaving home soon.

Family: Thank you father Tavaziva, Let us collect them. (The family are leaving their beautiful home).

Family: We will carry our clothes and walk to that bush which is surrounded by hills. All: Okay let us walk.

Tavaziva: We will put the clothes in one place.

Nyarai This is a good idea my husband. You leave us here and it's your duty to look for a vacancy. (When they were about to reach the place, the wife was asking her husband a way of getting food).

Nyarai: This is a nice place to camp, but where will we get food?

Tavaziva: If you want something to eat, you have to tell your sons to hunt for birds and seek wild fruits. (The man didn't stay for a long time in his camp)

Tavaziva: Now wife! I'm going sometime this afternoon.

Nyari: It's a good idea, you have to watch us here.

Tavaziva: "Good –bye-e- my family "(The lady decided to send her son Tigere to go hunting for the birds).

Nyarai: I'm hungry now, would you like to go hunting for birds?

Tigere: Yes, I'd like that and l will also look for wild fruits.

Nyarai:	Do you think you will find them?
Tigere:	I do hope l will. Good bye mother, Oh-oo- hey these are like wild oranges. (At that moment he ran to his mother holding a basket full of fruits).
Tigere:	Hii—let me run fast l have to do so. (The guy ran as fast as a hare chased by a dog).
Tigere:	I have reached the camp (calling) Mother! I am bringing you something to eat.
Nyarai:	Oh ---o! My son l like these fruits and l appreciate you a million times.

EPISODE 4
QUESTIONS TO ANSWER

1. Tavaziva was getting money from _____

   a. Vegetable sales
   b. Chicken sales.
   c. Fish sales.
   d. Cow sales

2. His family get food from_____

   a. Hunting birds and wild fruits
   b. Beer sales
   c. Work
   d. Friends

3. Who hold a basket full of fruits?

   a. Nyarai.
   b. Mother.
   c. Tigere
   d. Tavaziva.

4. Tigere was appreciated by whom?
   a. By her sister.
   b. By her brother.
   c. By her mother Nyarai.
   d. By her aunt.

UNDERSTANDING READING ADRAMA

EPISODE 5

Mr. Tavaziva At Chimusoro Farm

TAVAZIVA:	Now l am in Chimusoro farm and l fear for my family who are lonely in such dangerous bush. These days my ambition is to find work. If this happens I'll return to bring my family. I do know it is difficult to stay in such thick bush. (He saw an old man and called him).
TAVAZIVA:	Hey –e- you old man come here. (The old man's heart turned upside down, when he heard such a loud calling).
OLD MAN:	Hii- how; who is calling me this time? All the workers in this compound have left for their jobs, and l am staying alone with the little children.
TAVAZIVA:	Hey Old man don't you answer my call?
OLD MAN:	I heard you but I'm afraid to come to you.
TAVAZIVA:	I'd like to ask you something important, will you come?

OLD MAN:	Yes sir, I will come now (At that moment that old man walked on staggering to greet him).
OLDMAN:	Excuse me please Sir, how can l help you? It seems you are a stranger.
TAVAZIVA:	Yes, I'm a stranger but please will you show me the house of your Boss –boy.
OLDMAN:	I do hope you are an honest gentlemen l understand you. I can show his house. Do you see that big tree lying across the house?
TAVAZIVA:	Is that where he stays?
OLDMAN:	Yes it is.
TAVAZIVA:	Here is twenty dollars for you, you have helped me a lot, l appreciate you for your kind faith and l do hope l shall remember you if l meet you again. (When the man started walking he heard the children talking).
TAVAZIVA:	Who is making such a noise let me question them? Hey – you kids! Is the owner of this house around?
CHILDREN:	Do you mean our father?
TAVAZIVA:	Yes l do.
CHILDREN:	Will you wait for him he always comes here at twelve noon.
TAVAZIVA:	Thank you kid's l will wait for him.
CHILDREN:	Here comes father!
BOSS BOY:	How have you spent the day my children?
CHILDREN:	It was an exciting day but there is somebody outside the yard.
BOSS BOY:	Maybe this is a rascal wanting work in my yard. Let me call him, hey – you man come?

TAVAZIVA:	Excuse me sir for not greeting you. I do know l was bad mannered.
BOSS BOY:	What do you mean? l don't allow strangers to enter my farm.
TAVAZIVA:	Master l am looking for any kind of a vacancy.
BOSS BOY:	Wait here, l am looking for the number of workers l have in my record book.
TAVAZIVA:	If I get job l shall never drink anymore.
BOSS BOY:	You are in luck man, l am employing you as a general worker. I'd like you to start work tomorrow morning.
TAVAZIVA:	I will go to fetch my family just now.
BOSS BOY:	Where are they?
TAVAZIVA:	In the bush.
BOSS BOY:	(Laughing) Ha-ha-a-a! Go and do as l told you.
TAVAZIVA:	Good bye master, but if l reach the camp I will tell them to collect all clothes. Let me run as faster as l can. (The man arrived exactly at five o'clock at his camp).
TAVAZIVA:	How's life my wife Nyarai?
NYARAI:	We are suffering from hunger my husband Tavaziva, and l thought you were dead!
TAVAZIVA:	l am alive l confess things have been difficult.
NYARAI:	Children be kind! Don't you greet your father?
CHILDREN:	Okay mother we do greet him here comes father (Happily).
TAVAZIVA:	How are my children? I'm happy to see you today. How are you all?

CHILDREN:	We are fine and how are you too?
TAVAZIVA:	I am quite well.
NYARAI:	My husband Tavaziva you look happy! Did you get the job?
TAVAZIVA:	Oh – ah luckily l got the job at Chimusoro farm.
NYARAI:	Is it a nice farm Mr. Tavaziva.
TAVAZIVA:	It isn't so good, and I'm not interested in staying at such a farm.
NYARAI:	My husband l tell you this night. When a basin of water is suddenly tapped and brought back to its When a basin of water is suddenly tapped and brought back to its original position just as suddenly water will splash over the side moments after the action and the water will splash in the direction in which the action had taken place.
TAVAZIVA:	This is useful idea, and l didn't know that my wife Nyarai had such a big brain l hope you are able to control me Nyarai. I am telling you to carry all clothes, we are leaving the bush for our new house…
NYARAI:	This night my husband Tavaziva?
TAVAZIVA:	Yes.
NYARAI:	"Children" lets walk to our new house at Chimusoro farm.
CHILDREN:	Thank you mother.
NYARAI:	What is the time Mr. Tavaziva?
TAVAZIVA:	It is one o'clock.
NYARAI:	It's so dark, what if we meet snakes in these thick trees? Won't they bite us?

TAVAZIVA:	When you are on the way do not think such bad ideas just walk! As usual.
NYARAI:	It is better if l die than children, do you know that my husband?
TAVAZIVA:	I do know that! But don't you realize it is becoming bright.
NYARAI:	What makes it bright?
TAVAZIVA:	It's the stars.
NYARAI:	Let me count them, one, two, three, four and five.
TAVAZIVA:	Stare at me what sound are you making.
NYARAI:	I'm feeling as though l am masticating the sand in my mouth.
TAVAZIVA:	Close your mouth and do not think about anything.
NYARAI:	I won't close it, I'm hearing some cocks crowing.
TAVAZIVA:	We are about to reach the farm, but l would like to tell you before we arrive at home, that when a person suddenly entered a dimly lighted room from strong sunlight it takes a little time before that person can see anything. The eye must adjust itself to the changed light conditions.
NYARAI:	"Light" what does this tale mean?
TAVAZIVA:	It means if you reach out house, it is different from the bush. You do meet many ladies but do not be friendly with them at that moment. First study their situation and culture before you join them, then after knowing their habits then you are able to join them.
Nyarai:	I shall obey your advice my husband Tavaziva. It will stand out in my heart. (The family had arrived at the farm and let's see the boss boy welcome them).

TAVAZIVA:	Do you see that gentlemen looking at us? That is our Boss from today.
NYARAI:	Yes l do see him and he seems a respectable man.
BOSS BOY:	Welcome my beloved relation in work! This is the house in which you will stay and start the job this morning. (Politely). It's exciting to have such a fascinating house and l do appreciate our master for his kind deeds.

EPISODE 5
QUESTIONS TO ANSWER

1. Tavaziva get the job at_____

    a. Chimusoro farm.
    b. Kananda farm.
    c. Jongwe farm.
    d. Chikaka farm.

2. Who called an old man?

    a. An old man was called by Tavaziva.
    b. An old man was called by Nyarai.
    c. An old man was called by the Boss.
    d. An old man was called by children.

3. How much money do Tavaziva give to the helper?

    a. He gave one dollar.
    b. He gave five dollars.
    c. He gave ten dollars.
    d. He gave twenty dollars.

4. Nyarai obeyed advice from_____

    a. Her children
    b. Her sister.
    c. Her friends
    d. Her husband Tavaziva.

UNDERSTANDING READING A DRAMA

EPISODE 6

Mr. Tavaziva starts working

TAVAZIVA: Good bye! My family l am going to start the job this morning. I shall see you in the afternoon.

FAMILY: Good bye father; (When the man reached the work he waited for the boss boy).

TAVAZIVA: Good morning Sir,

BOSS BOY: Good morning and how are you? Do you want to work with my group?

TAVAZIVA: Yes l do…

BOSS BOY: Our usual work at this farm is to shovel the river sand

TAVAZIVA: It seems like a difficult work, master.

BOSS BOY: Yes it is very hard work but what can l do for you?

TAVAZIVA: Will you give me that shovel please master?

BOSS BOY: You do agree do this job? Here is the shovel.

TAVAZIVA: Today is very cold, if l start working l will feel hot. (The man was working very hard and he was appreciated by his master).

BOSS BOY: We need strong men like you here, and l am allowing you to go home and have food. You will start your work tomorrow morning.

TAVAZIVA: (Politely) Thank you master. The man started walking on staggering and emphasizing being exhausted.

TAVAZIVA: l worked hard today, sweat and dust are entering my eyes. I am also unable to walk, the penalty of my goal is to suffer for my family my son Tigere is able to find for him a job l can't stay together with such a big boy. I would like to look after my wife Nyarai and these two small children, Tapera and Chipo. Once l reach home will gather my family and tell them interesting tale. (When he arrived at home his wife and children welcomed him).

FAMILY: Welcome father!

TAVAZIVA: Ho-o-yes my family l am very tired l need some drinking water.

NYARAI: Tapera! Fetch cold water and give to your father.

TAPERA: (Politely) Okay, mother here's the water father.

TAVAZIVA: (With a pale face) thank you my son.

NYARAI: Shall l bring food for you my husband?

TAVAZIVA: Before l eat the food l want all of you to gather here, and l want tell you an interesting tale. (All of them are gathered and waited to hear the story from him).

TAVAZIVA: I'm telling you this, the more you earn the more money is needed to pay food to keep all together. (The family is silent in hearing a strange tale).

FAMILY: How! What does this tale meant? Let us not guess.

Nyarai: My husband, may l bring you food please?

TAVAZIVA: Yes, l do need to eat together with my children. Call them. (Children eat together with your father).

TIGERE: No, thank you father l have had enough. (Tigere refused food).

EPISODE 6

QUESTIONS TO ANSWER

1. Tavaziva's job was to_____

    a. Shovel river sand.
    b. Dig the gardener
    c. Cut the tree.
    d. General worker.

2. How many children has Tavaziva?

    a. He had one child.
    b. He had two children.
    c. He had three children.
    d. He had four children.

3. Who refused the food?
4.
    a. Was Tapera.
    b. Was Chipo.
    c. Was Nyarai.
    d. Was Tigere.

5. The children were listening a tale from their _____

    a. Father.
    b. Mother.
    c. Uncle
    d. Aunt.

UNDERSTANDING READING A DRAMA
EPISODE 7

A Wondering Son

TIGERE: My parents do not like me, also the world hates me my clothes are tattered and nobody is providing with food l am facing many troubles alone. (After speaking he has some important ideas).

TIGERE: l am having a very difficult life. I know that a person does not wait for somebody to change him. It's my ambition to do something which guides me to a good life. (Tigere is a small boy but his effort is to find a job).

TIGERE: l know that l am a very small boy, if l find a job those who hate me will be ashamed. I have to find it quickly and l don't want anybody to know my future plans. In our situation if somebody does well everybody resents it. (In the morning he started his journey to an unknown place. His parents were asleep on their beds and he kept to his plan and started to look for work).

TIGERE: (Thinking) l am leaving my parents now, the weather is too cold. It makes all fish asleep in the rivers. As l am walking l will not take anything from this home l shall travel single. I still remember the proverb which says, "Suffering is nothing so long life, and a half loaf is better than none". (Whilst he was on his way to unknown place, he met a Herdsman Hey -, hii—me-ee, l hear the moos of the cows, who's herding the cattle? Is there somebody around here? O-oo yes l see a herdsman let me run to him. To shy doesn't make a person successful even if he scolds me l will be silent. (The herdsman heard the movement of the soil then hesitated)

HERDSMAN: What makes a noise like a lion! Let me stare in that direction. Hii-I Hey – l can see a dwarf person coming towards me. I will wait here he arrives. (When the boy reached the herdsman he took off his hat and grasped his hand.

HERDSMAN: It seems you are a mad person why do you grasp me! and your clothing is dirty! Tigere: I was afraid of being lonely in such thick bush. As l am a young motivated guy, l am looking for any kind of job.

HERDSMAN: l am the owner of these cattle and l am looking for a young guy like you to do this job. I will pay you twenty dollars each Friday, l also provide you with some food and clothes.

TIGERE: Working for small money! Where will I be staying master?

MASTER: You will be staying together with my family in a beautiful palace.

TIGERE: What is the name of the village where you stay?

MASTER: It is called Jongwe village and l am the kraal herdsman there.

TIGERE: I do like the work, l do hope it will interest me if you are employing me l first want to know the day l will start work.

MASTER: "You start the job just now, do you see these donkeys? You will be riding on them when you begin herding these cattle.

TIGERE: You will train me please master?

MASTER: l will train you today and during the weekend.

TIGERE: I'd like to visit your house before l begin the work.

MASTER: Ok we will go very soon, but we will not walk fast, we use these donkeys on our journey home.

TIGERE: (Smiling) that's a good idea to use them in case if we walk on foot we take a long time to reach the village (Tigere is happy because it is his first ride on a donkey. Now let's watch them on their way home).

MASTER: Donkeys are the most useful animal here in Zimbabwe.

TIGERE: Is it the meat fit for eating?

MASTER: (Laughing) Ha-aha-aa!!) l don't eat them, but in other countries such as Arabia they use the camels as their ship on a desert and for meat and milk. Here in Zimbabwe l love the donkeys so much because l use them for carrying my bags of dry maize, ground nuts, herding the cattle and for ploughing my fields.

Tigere: Why are we using these animals for our journey home?

Master: Do you see lots of thorns in these forest if we walk on foot wont they prick our feet?

TIGERE: Yes, they will get inside our feet.

MASTER: You better know that, although we are travelling on them it doesn't mean we are rich or lazy. Some of the people in our village are poor.

TIGERE: l do not understand your speech Master, you said you were poor although you have many cattle and your own fields. I judge you to be a great rich man in your village.

MASTER: Being rich doesn't make a person happy. I am always sad to confess as many troubles. If you are poor you do no need to buy expensive food and clothes.

TIGERE: Like me I am very poor everything goes the wrong way. "Look"! Master, your donkey is walking majestically. It shows me that the world is moving well for you.

MASTER: (Blaming him) you thin dwarf person! It is your first ride on donkey and l tell you this foolish people are those who are shy to do something which might lead them to a better road.

TIGERE: Does this mean I'm foolish to have to work for you and not have any field?

MASTER: (In a laughter) yes, you are really foolish and you don't have anywhere to go your life will be here.

TIGERE: You do mean l shall work for you until l die.

MASTER: Yes that is my idea.

TIGERE: (Scolding) it won't happen here in Zimbabwe. I'm not crazy! i do know my future life.

MASTER: We are about to reach home and be quiet.

TIGERE: How far is it?

MASTER: its a hundred yards.

TIGERE: l can see some beautiful houses.

MASTER: That is my village and how beautiful are those houses?

TIGERE: Very beautiful! (The fellows are happy because their journey is over).

MASTER: We have reached my house and let's get off our donkeys, and l would like to feed them with some sweets and bread.

Tigere: It's an exciting idea to give them food, because these animals are hungry they have not eaten anything since this morning.

RED BIRD: Good bye to all audience. I am flying off to Great Zimbabwe and l shall meet you again here in Harare.

EPISODE 7
QUESTIONS TO ANSWER

1. Why Tigere leave his parents?

    a. Because he was rejected.
    b. Because he was hated.
    c. Because he was unloved.
    d. Because he was hated by the world.

2. What time did Tigere start his journey?

    a. He started in the morning.
    b. He started in the afternoon.
    c. He started in the evening.
    d. He started at dawn.

1. The two proverbs named in the passage by Tigere are
   _____ and _____

    a. Blood is thicker than water.
    b. Suffering is nothing so long life and a half loaf is better than none.
    c. There is many way to kill a cat.
    d. Talkative is an empty bucket.

3. Tigere leaved in_____
    a. Kananda Village.
    b. Jongwe Village.
    c. Chimusoro Village.
    d. Chikwakwa Village.

SUPPLEMENTARY DICTIONARY

Word	Meaning
Ancestor	the spirit of fore father and mother
Ashamed	feeling shame
Behold	keep in the hand
Blame	find a fault with
Certainly	something certain
Confess	acknowledge
Crazy	mad
Croak	as a frog
Crow	as a cock
Dim	not bright
Dismiss	allow to go
Disobey	refuse to obey
Dropped	fall
Dwarf	abnormally small person
Effort	mental power
Emphasize	lay stress upon
Enthusiastic	interest
Entrance	place of entering

Exhausted	-	used up completely
Expensive	-	costly
Fanfare	-	flourish played on trumpets.
Fascinate	-	attract and hold irresistible
Fetch	-	to go and bring
Figured	-	character
Grasped	-	seize and holding with the fingers.
Grim	-	cruel
Hesitated	-	hold back in doubt Hid - keep secret
Hillock	-	little hill
Hum	-	make a low
Impressed	-	effort deeply
Intruded	-	to enter without invited or welcome.
Knelt	-	rest on the knee
Majestically	-	imposing
Masticate	-	chew
Microscope	-	combination of lenses for inspecting objects too small to be seen in a detail.
Moos	-	as a cow sound
Motivate	-	something that prompts a person to act.
Obey	-	listen

Original	-	the beginning first
Palace	-	official residence of a sovereign, a bishop
Pale	-	without intensity of colour
Pathway	-	as under pain.
Patter	-	move with slight tapping sound.
Peeped	-	look through a small apertures
Penalty	-	punishment for a violation law
Politely	-	showing good manner
Provide	-	supply
Rascal	-	dishonest person
Recognize	-	perceive to be identical with something previously known.
Relish	-	for the taste of something.
Research	-	investigate carefully
Resent	-	feel
Roar	-	as a lion sound
Rum	-	alcoholic liquor
Shyly	-	as in fear
Situation	-	condition
Splash	-	mud
Stagger	-	to go swaying

Starred	-	fixed look
Sting	-	sharp printed organ of inserts and other animals.
Stranger	-	newcomer in a place
Stuck	-	to stick up.
Suddenly	-	happening
Tale	-	narrative about some events.
Tattered	-	torn piece
Tapped	-	wigwam
Terrible	-	bad
Thatched	-	to cover roofs
Thicket	-	covered
Thorn	-	tree or flick plant
Tip	–	toe- move on tip toe
Tremble	-	quiver, as from fear, cold.
Wondering place	-	nomadic or one moving from one place to another

RECOMMENDATIONS

Another Kind of Poverty invaluable recommendations made by a famous author, teachers, various publishers such as;

LONGMAN ZIMBABWE, BAOBAB BOOKS ZIMBABWE and HEINEMAN BOOKS AFRICA had under gone assessment for the pupils' drama Book.

RECOMMENDATIONS

These drama stories offer interesting reading matter for pupils of English as second or fore in Language who have reached a stage between the graded supplementary reader and full simplified English.

The idea in this drama book is impressed and also fairly good. The drama stories could be suitable used in a school class performed from grades three to seven. At the end of each chapter there are questions to